GW00360487

SAINT THÉRÈSE OF LISIEUX
The Little Flower

JACK O'NEILL

Saint Thérèse of Lisieux
The Little Flower

Illustrations by
Kati Teague

ST PAULS

Other titles in this series:

St Paul – Friend of Jesus
St John Vianney – The Curé of Ars
Blessed John Henry Newman – Heart Speaks to Heart

ST PAULS Publishing
187 Battersea Bridge Road, London SW11 3AS, UK
www.stpaulspublishing.com

A catalogue record is available for this book from
the British Library.

Set by TuKan DTP, Stubbington, Fareham, UK
Printed through s|s|media, Wallington, Surrey

ST PAULS is an activity of the priests and brothers
of the Society of St Paul who proclaim the Gospel
through the media of social communication.

Introduction

Many, many years ago a watchmaker and his wife lived in a little house in the French town of Alençon. His name was Louis Martin. His wife was called Zèlie and she was a lacemaker.

They lived with their four daughters, Marie, Pauline, Leonie and Céline.

On 2nd January 1873, on a cold winter's night, the soft cry of a new-born baby girl was heard.

Louis and Zèlie smiled at their newborn daughter and named her Marie François Thérèse Martin. That was a big name for such a little girl, so they called her simply Thérèse. Thérèse's mother wrapped her baby warmly and held her close. She was worried that Thérèse might die because, although Thérèse had four older healthy sisters, Zèlie also had given birth to two baby boys and two baby girls who had died when they were young. Zèlie was very worried, so she prayed to God that Thérèse would live and grow up to be strong and healthy.

Thérèse grew into a pretty, happy child with long golden hair. Her mother, father and sisters loved her very much, and Thérèse liked to please them. Thérèse laughed a lot and was treated as a little queen by her family. She liked their attention and her golden curls would bounce as she played in the house and the garden. But Thérèse was also very stubborn and always wanted to get her own way.

Her mother once said that when Thérèse said 'No', then nothing would change her mind.

Thérèse would always say what she thought, and liked to be able to have everything she wanted. One day her sister Leonie brought a basket of dolls and toys to Thérèse and Céline. Leonie asked her little sisters what things would they like to choose. Céline chose a ball, but Thérèse, with a mischievous grin on her face, said 'I choose all' and took the whole basket.

Everyone was happy in the Martin house. Louis and Zèlie were good parents and Thérèse loved her sisters. However, the happiness was not to last. Thérèse's mother became very ill and died of cancer when Thérèse was only four-and-a-half years old. The five sisters stood together after the funeral and felt very sad because they had lost their mother. Céline ran to her older sister Marie and asked her if she would now be her mother.

Thérèse ran to Pauline and asked
her the same question. Leonie
looked on with a smile and
the sisters hugged each
other and promised
to care for each
other.

Louis Martin was worried about how he could look after his five daughters on his own, so he decided to move to the town of Lisieux where Thérèse's aunt and uncle lived. He bought a house, which they called 'Les Buissonnets' because it was surrounded by 'little bushes'.

The sisters loved their new home with the beautiful little garden. They also liked being near to their aunt, uncle and cousins, but they were still sad that their mother had died, especially Thérèse.

Thérèse was no longer the bouncy, noisy child she used to be; she often cried and became a sad little girl. Toys, games and things around her were not so important to her any more.

She spent more and more time thinking about her mother in heaven with Jesus, whom she was beginning to know and love as a friend, and wanted to be with them. She asked Jesus to help her to be good and kind so that one day she also would to go to heaven. She would often go for walks in the countryside with her father and, as he was fishing, she would sit among the flowers and dream of heaven.

When Thérèse was eight years old she went to school in Lisieux where the teachers were nuns. Thérèse was clever at school and did well in her tests but she was not good at games. She found it difficult to make friends and some of the older girls teased her and were so cruel that she cried.

Thérèse was not happy at school and she would often spend time sitting by herself. When the nuns asked what she was thinking about she told them that she thought about God.

A year later her older sister Pauline told her that she was going to leave and become a nun in a convent called the Carmel. Once again Thérèse was losing someone special to her. She felt very alone, very sad and soon became so ill that she had to stay in bed. The whole family were worried about her and the doctor did not know how to make her better. Céline and Leonie knelt down in the bedroom before a statue of Mary, the mother of Jesus, and started to pray that their little sister would recover.

As Thérèse looked over at the statue, it seemed to move. Then, as the face of Mary smiled at Thérèse, she felt better and her heart was no longer sad.

Thérèse realised that she became sad only when she could not have the things she wanted. She wanted her mother – but her mother had died. She wanted her sister Pauline – but Pauline had left home to live in the Carmel. So Thérèse decided that she would try to stop wanting things and concentrate on Jesus and heaven. She realised that if she copied Jesus by trying to be good and kind to others, then one day she would be with him in heaven, and make other people happy by her kindness.

Thérèse made her First Holy Communion when she was eleven years old and it was such a very special day for her. She realised that she would be able to receive Jesus in Holy Communion and he would enter even more closely into her heart. After her First Holy Communion she was very happy and went to the Carmel to see her sister Pauline.

Thérèse was no longer sad that her
sister was in the Carmel because
she felt that Jesus was asking
her to become a nun, like Pauline.
Thérèse wanted to spend her
life in prayer and to become even
closer to Jesus.

As time went on Thérèse spent more and more time praying and talking to Jesus. She believed that she could help people by praying for them and that if she prayed for people then miracles could happen, because God wants the best for us. One day Thérèse heard about a criminal who had killed people and was not sorry for what he had done.

Thérèse was worried that the man would not be able to go to heaven if he was not sorry for doing wrong, so every day she prayed for him.

The time came when the man was about to die, but just before he died he reached out and kissed a cross, which is the symbol of Jesus' love for everyone. When Thérèse heard about this she knew that her prayers had been answered and that a miracle had happened. Thérèse decided that she wanted to spend her life praying for other people,

When Thérèse was fourteen years old her sister Marie told her that she was going to be a nun and live in the Carmel, just like Pauline. Thérèse wanted to join them, but her father said she was too young and had to wait until she was sixteen years old. Thérèse begged her father because she did not want to wait any longer.

As her father listened to her, he picked
up a little white flower and gave it to her.
Thérèse saw that the little flower still had
roots on it and realised that she was like
the little flower – she would leave her
home and be 'planted' to grow in
the Carmel. Her father then
said yes, she could become
a nun.

Even though her father agreed to let Thérèse become a nun, the priest in charge of the Carmel said that Thérèse was too young and she would have to wait even longer, until she was twenty-one years old.

Thérèse went to ask the Bishop, but he also said she was too young. There was only one other person who would be able to let her become a nun at such a young age and that was the Pope who lived in Rome.

Thérèse went to Rome with her father to see the Pope. She begged the Pope to allow her to become a nun in the Carmel even though she was only fifteen years old.

He smiled at the young girl and told her that if God wished her to become a nun then that would happen, but she must do what the Bishop told her to do.

Thérèse was sad, but realised that she had done everything she could and she decided to trust in Jesus and do as she was told.

A few weeks after Thérèse returned to Lisieux from Rome, she received a letter from the Bishop. He had changed his mind and agreed that she could become a nun and live in the Carmel. Thérèse was so happy. The day finally came when her father brought Thérèse to the Carmel. Her sisters opened the door and she was welcomed to live there with the other nuns.

Thérèse saw the little room where she would sleep with the tiny bed and chair. She looked around her and she smiled. This would be her home and she would spend her life trying her hardest to be good and to pray for others.

Thérèse Martin was given a new name when she became a nun. Her new name was Sister Thérèse of the Child Jesus.

Thérèse's new life was not an easy one. The nuns lived very simply without comfortable things, taking special care of each other and praying for the people outside the convent who asked for their help. There was no choice of food and they had to eat what they were given. The nuns got up at 5 a.m. to pray and spent a total of six hours during the day praying in the church.

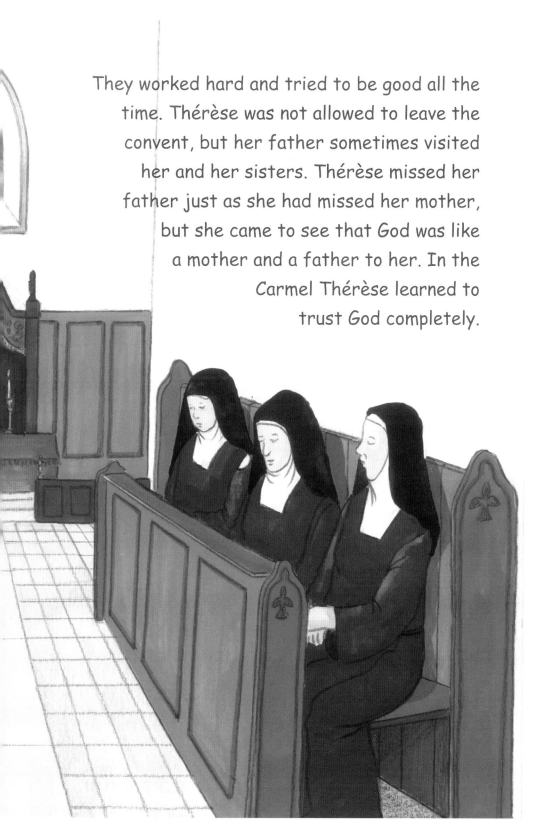

They worked hard and tried to be good all the time. Thérèse was not allowed to leave the convent, but her father sometimes visited her and her sisters. Thérèse missed her father just as she had missed her mother, but she came to see that God was like a mother and a father to her. In the Carmel Thérèse learned to trust God completely.

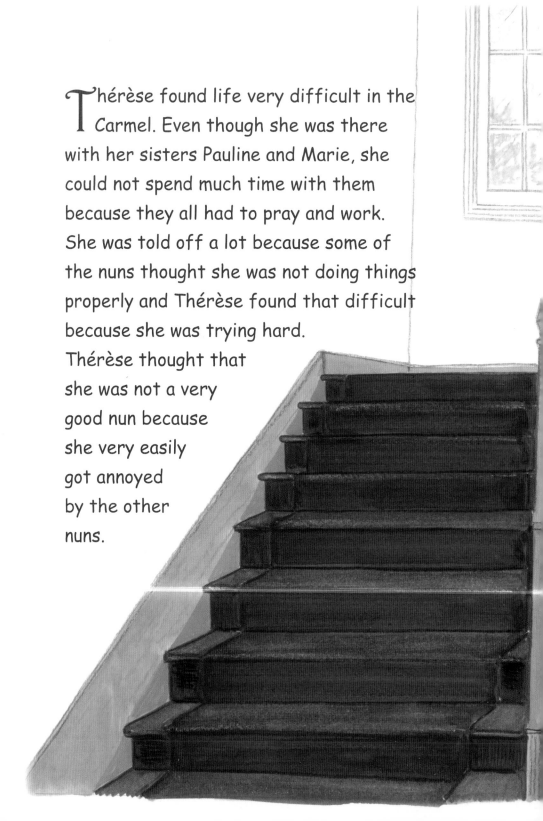

Thérèse found life very difficult in the Carmel. Even though she was there with her sisters Pauline and Marie, she could not spend much time with them because they all had to pray and work. She was told off a lot because some of the nuns thought she was not doing things properly and Thérèse found that difficult because she was trying hard.

Thérèse thought that she was not a very good nun because she very easily got annoyed by the other nuns.

She decided to try her very best to be kind and generous, and to love all those around her the way Jesus loved them. Even if someone was not being nice, Thérèse tried to find something nice about them.

Thérèse wanted Jesus to be happy with her in this life and dreamed of going to heaven when she died. She thought that it was so very difficult to be a saint and that she was not strong enough or good enough to be like them. Sometimes she even fell asleep in church and felt bad about that too.

Thérèse thought that trying to be a saint was like climbing a difficult path to heaven. She needed to find a better way of getting there – like getting into a lift instead of having to climb the stairs.

Thérèse thought she would not be able to do wonderful things like the saints. So she decided to try to love Jesus and help other people in her own "Little Way". Thérèse's "Little Way" was that every day she would try to do things to help the other nuns, even when she found it difficult. She made friends and helped even the nuns she did not like. Thérèse did jobs that other nuns did not want to do and, even if they were not nice to her, she would smile and be nice to them.

It was hard for Thérèse to be nice all the time to everyone, but she knew that all she had to do was welcome Jesus into her heart and he would be kind to people through her.

Thérèse would try to do lots of little good things every day, that way she could become like the saints, even if people did not notice her good things.

She thought of herself as being like the little white flower her father once gave her and that Jesus would care for her. Then, in turn, she could try each day to love everyone and to pray for them and do nice things to make people happy.

Thérèse knew that Jesus loved her as a 'little flower' because she loved people in small, but beautiful, ways.

She had read in
the Bible that
Jesus loves little
children because
they are simple
and trusting, and
Thérèse wanted to
be like that too.

As time passed, the other nuns at the Carmel saw how kind and good Thérèse was becoming. They didn't know about many of the little things she used to do to be kind and to help, although they noticed some of them.

One day Thérèse's sister, Pauline, asked her to write about her life and memories so that they could remember their lives as children and not forget. Thérèse sat in her little room and wrote down all the things she remembered and about how she tried to become close to God and be good.

Thérèse gave the story of her life to her sister and continued to try to live her simple and good life in the Carmel. However, when Pauline read what Thérèse had written she knew that Thérèse had found a good way to live the sort of life that Jesus wanted.

She showed the story to the nun in charge of the Carmel. They asked Thérèse to write some more so that people could read it and they could copy Thérèse living her "Little Way" to God.

Living in the Carmel was difficult because it was so cold and Thérèse began to get sick. She carried on trying to live a good life and practice her "Little Way" of doing good things every day without complaining. As time passed she became more and more ill. Eventually, she could not carry on with her jobs in the Carmel and had to stay in bed.

Thérèse had an illness called tuberculosis, which
was a sickness in her lungs and very painful.
Even though she was so ill and in pain, she did
not complain and tried to make the
other nuns laugh
and smile when
they came to
see her.

The illness got worse and Thérèse realised she was going to die. One of the nuns asked her if she was afraid of dying, but Thérèse said that she was happy because she would be able to help people even more by praying for them from heaven. She said her help would fall from heaven like a shower of roses.

In the last few months of her life Thérèse was in a lot of pain. She still did not complain but always tried to be brave and kind and always trusted in her friend Jesus to bring her to heaven. Finally, on 30th September 1897, when Thérèse was still only 24 years old, she died.

After Thérèse died the nuns made a book out of the stories she wrote about her life and how she tried to live her "Little Way" of being good. They called the book ***The Story of a Soul***. A lot of people read the book and it taught them how to live a good life too. Soon, Thérèse was famous all over the world because of the way she tried to live.

People said prayers to her to ask her to help them from heaven by telling God about their hopes and troubles. Lots of people believed that when they read her story and asked Thérèse to help them, miracles happened and she did help them. They described these miracles as a shower of roses falling from heaven. Each petal was a miracle where Thérèse helped them.

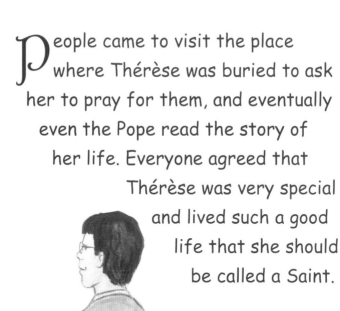

People came to visit the place where Thérèse was buried to ask her to pray for them, and eventually even the Pope read the story of her life. Everyone agreed that Thérèse was very special and lived such a good life that she should be called a Saint.

On 17th May 1925 the Pope told everyone that from that day forward Thérèse was going to be called "Saint Thérèse of the Child Jesus". Many people also remember her as Saint Thérèse of Lisieux, but most people call her **The Little Flower**, just like the little flower her father gave to her on the day she told him she wanted to become a nun in the Carmel. The Pope said that Thérèse's parents were such good people that they are in heaven too. Saint Thérèse carries on helping people, and her shower of roses continues to fall from heaven to this day.